Financial ‿

An Entrepreneurs Guide on Mastering the Game of Money and Building Real Financial Freedom in Business

Volume 2: Financial Statements

By

Income Mastery

In addition, the information on the following pages is intended for informational purposes only and should therefore be regarded as universal. As befits its nature, it is presented without warranty with respect to its prolonged validity or provisional quality. The trademarks mentioned are made without written consent and can in no way be considered as sponsorship of the same.

Table of Contents

Chapter I: What is financial intelligence?

Financial intelligence is the gathering of information about the financial affairs of entities of interest, so as to understand their nature and capabilities, and to predict their intentions. In general, the term applies in the context of law enforcement and related activities.

One of the main purposes of financial intelligence is to identify financial transactions that may involve tax evasion, money laundering or other criminal activity. It can also participate in identifying financing for criminal and terrorist organizations.

Financial intelligence can be divided into two main areas, **collection and analysis**. The collection is normally done by a government agency, known as a financial intelligence organization or Financial Intelligence Unit (FIU). The agency will collect raw transactional information and suspicious activity reports (SARs), generally provided by banks and other entities, as part of regulatory requirements. Data can be shared with other countries through intergovernmental networks.

Analysis can consist of scrutinizing a large volume of transactional data using data mining or data comparison techniques to identify people potentially involved in a particular activity. SARs can also be analyzed and linked to other data to try to identify specific activities.

- **Harvesting**

Financial intelligence involves scrutiny of a large volume of transactional data, usually provided by banks and other entities as part of regulatory requirements. Alternatively, data mining or data matching techniques can be employed to identify persons potentially involved in a particular activity.

Many industrialized countries have regulatory reporting requirements for their financial organizations.

Such an organization may have access to data that hasn't been processed by a financial organization. From a legal point of view, this type of collection can be quite complex. For example, the CIA gained access to data flows from the Society for Worldwide Interbank Financial Telecommunications (SWIFT) through the Terrorist Finance Tracking Programme, but this violated Belgian privacy law.

Reporting requirements may not affect informal value transfer systems (IVTS), whose use may simply be customary in a culture, and amounts that would not require reporting in a conventional financial institution. IVTS may also be used for criminal purposes to avoid supervision.

- **Analysis**

Examples of financial intelligence analysis might include:

✓ Identifying tenants of high-risk housing based on past rental histories.

✓ Detecting taxpayers trying to avoid their fiduciary duties by surreptitiously transferring wealth from a tax-collecting jurisdiction.

✓ Discovering safe havens where criminals park the proceeds of crime.

✓ Counting how a large sum of money given to a target individual disappears.

✓ Checking to see if a corrupt individual has had unexpected, sudden and unexplained gains.

✓ Detecting relationships between terrorist cells through remittances.

Financial intelligence organizations

According to the Egmont Financial Intelligence Units Group, financial intelligence organizations (FIUs) are national centers that collect information on suspicious or unusual financial activities of the financial industry and other entities or professions required to report transactions suspected of being money laundering or terrorist financing. FIUs are not normally law enforcement agencies; their mission is to process and analyze the information received. If sufficient evidence of illegal activity is found, the matter is referred to the prosecutor's office.

Government organizations can simply receive and process gross financial reports, and send them, as appropriate, to intelligence or law enforcement agencies, including the multinational Egmont Group of Financial Intelligence Units and national organizations, which include:

- ✓ Argentina - Financial Intelligence Unit.

- ✓ Australia - Australian Transaction Analysis and Reporting Centre (AUSTRAC).

- ✓ Brazil - COAF Financial Activity Control Council.

- ✓ Canada - Financial Transaction Analysis and Reporting Centre of Canada (FINTRAC).

- ✓ France – Tracfin.

- ✓ Alemania - Central Office for Financial Transaction Investigations.

- ✓ India - Financial Intelligence Unit (FIU-IND).

- ✓ Ireland - Garda Financial Intelligence Unit (FIU GNECB).

- ✓ United Kingdom - National Crime Agency.

✓ United States - Financial Crimes Enforcement Network (FinCEN).

Let's take a look at the Financial Crimes Enforcement Network (FinCEN).

It is an office of the U.S. Ministry of Economy that collects and analyzes information on financial transactions to combat domestic and international money laundering, terrorist financing and other financial crimes.

Mission Statement

The director of FinCEN expressed his mission in November 2013 as "protecting the financial system from illicit use, combating money laundering and promoting national security." FinCEN serves as the U.S. Financial Intelligence Unit (FIU) and is one of 147 FIUs that make up the Egmont Group of Financial Intelligence Units. FinCEN's self-described motto is "Follow the money". The website says: "The main motive of criminals is financial gain, and they leave financial footprints while trying to launder the proceeds of crime or spend their illegally earned gains." It is a network that brings people and information together, coordinating the exchange of information with law enforcement agencies, regulators and other partners in the financial industry.

History

FinCEN was established by order of the Secretary of the Ministry of Economy (Orden Ministerio de Economía Numerada 105-08) on April 25, 1990. In May, 1994, its mission was expanded to include regulatory responsibilities, and in October 1994 the forerunner of the Ministry of Economy, FinCEN, the Financial Compliance Office, merged with FinCEN. On September 26, 2002, after the approval of Title III of the Patriot Act, the Order Ministry of Economy 180-01, made it an official office of the Ministry of Economy. In September 2012, FinCEN's information technology, called FinCEN Portal and Query System, migrated with 11 years of data to FinCEN Query, a search engine similar to Google. It is a "one-stop shop" accessible through the FinCEN Portal, which allows people to perform extensive searches in more fields than before and obtain more results. Since September 2012 FinCEN generates 4 new reports: Suspicious Activity Report (FinCEN SAR), Monetary Transaction Report (FinCEN CTR), Exempt Person Designation (DOEP) and Registered Money Services Business (RMSB).

Organization

As of November 2013, FinCEN employed approximately 340 individuals, mostly intelligence professionals with experience in the financial industry, illicit finance, financial intelligence, AML/CFT regulatory regime (money laundering/ terrorism financing), information technology and enforcement. The majority of the staff is permanent FinCEN staff, with about 20 long-term detainees assigned from 13 different regulatory and law enforcement agencies. FinCEN shares information with dozens of intelligence agencies, including the Bureau of Alcohol, Tobacco, and Firearms; the Drug Enforcement Administration; the Federal Bureau of Investigation; the U.S. Secret Service; the Internal Revenue Service; the Customs Service; and the U.S. Postal Inspection Service.

Examples from the United States

The United States has different organizations focused on domestic and international financial activity. The United States has several laws that require reporting to FinCEN.

These include the Financial Privacy Rights Act (RFPA) of 1978, the Bank Secrecy Act of 1970 (and other names of revisions) and the Gramm - Leach - Bliley Act of 1999 (GLBA). Some reports must also go to the Securities and Exchange Commission.

For example, the following reports:

Report and definition	Authority	Receiving agency
Currency Transaction Report (CTR). Cash transactions in excess of $10,000 during the same business day. Amounts greater than $10,000 may be from one transaction or a combination of cash transactions.	Bank Secrecy Act	Internal Revenue Service
Registration of negotiable instruments (NIL). Cash purchases of negotiable instruments (e.g., drafts, cashier's checks, traveler's checks) having a face value of $3,000 or more.	Bank Secrecy Act	Internal Revenue Service

Suspicious Activity Report (SAR). Any cash transaction in which the customer appears to be trying to avoid BSA reporting requirements (e.g., CTR, NIL). A SAR must also be filed if the client's actions indicate that he or she is laundering money or violating the federal criminal law. The client should not know that a SAR is being filed.	Bank Secrecy Act	Financial Crimes Enforcement Network

Actions that may trigger the filing of a Suspicious Activity Report (SAR) include:

1. Any type of internal abuse of a financial institution, involving any amount of money.

2. Federal offenses against or involving transactions conducted through a financial institution that the financial institution detects and that involve at least

$5,000 if a suspect can be identified, or at least $25,000 regardless of whether a suspect can be identified.

3. Transactions of at least $5,000 that the institution knows, suspects, or has reason to suspect involve funds from illegal activities or are structured to attempt to conceal those funds.

4. Transactions of at least $5,000 that the institution knows, suspects or has reason to suspect are designed to evade any regulation enacted under the Bankruptcy Secrecy Act.

5. Transactions of at least $5,000 that the institution knows, suspects or has reason to suspect have no apparent business or legal purpose or are not of the type in which the particular customer would normally be expected to participate, and for which the institution knows no reasonable explanation after due investigation. The PFP language indicates that a Suspicious Activity Report filed under this rule comes from an individual transaction, not from a profile of activities that make the transaction stand out.

U.S. National Financial Intelligence (FININT)

At the highest level, the U.S. national FININT, as well as some international assignments, report to the Undersecretary of the Ministry of Economy for

Terrorism and Financial Intelligence, head of the Terrorism and Financial Analysis Bureau, which includes:

- ✓ **Financial Crimes Enforcement Network**: tracks domestic transactions

- ✓ **Office of Foreign Assets Control (OFAC)**: focused on foreign assets in the U.S.

It is a financial intelligence and enforcement agency of the U.S. Department of the Economy that administers and enforces economic and trade sanctions in support of U.S. national security and foreign policy objectives. Under national emergency presidential powers, OFAC conducts its activities against foreign states, as well as against a variety of other organizations and individuals, such as terrorist groups, considered a threat to the U.S. national security.

As a component of the U.S. Department of the Economy, OFAC operates under the Office of Terrorism and Financial Intelligence and is composed primarily of intelligence targets and lawyers. While many of OFAC's objectives are widely established by the White House, most individual cases are developed as a result of investigations by OFAC's Office of Global Guidance (OGT).

Sometimes described as one of the "most powerful but unknown" government agencies, OFAC was founded in 1950 and has the power to impose significant sanctions against entities that defy its directives, including imposing fines, freezing assets and prohibiting parties from operating in the United States. In 2014, OFAC reached a record deal of $963 million with the French bank BNP Paribas, which was part of an $8.9 billion fine imposed on the case as a whole.

Authorities and activities

In addition to the Enemy Trade Act and the various national emergencies currently in effect, OFAC derives its authority from a variety of U.S. federal embargo and economic sanctions laws.

In enforcing economic sanctions, OFAC acts to prevent "prohibited transactions," which OFAC describes as "commercial or financial transactions and other dealings in which Americans may not participate unless authorized by OFAC or expressly exempted by law." OFAC has the authority to grant exemptions from the prohibitions on such transactions, either by issuing a general license for certain categories of transactions, or by issuing specific licenses on a case-by-case basis. OFAC administers and implements economic sanctions programs against countries, companies or groups of people, using asset freezing and trade restrictions to achieve foreign policy and national security objectives. See the U.S. embargoes for a list of affected countries.

Under the International Emergency Economic Powers Act (IEEPA), the President of the United States is empowered during domestic emergencies to block the disposal of foreign assets under the U.S. jurisdiction. OFAC executes this mandate by issuing regulations that direct financial institutions accordingly.

Between 1994 and 2003, OFAC raised more than $8 million in violations of the Cuban embargo, against just under $10,000 for terrorist financing violations. He had ten times more agents assigned to track financial activities related to Cuba than Osama Bin Laden.

As part of its efforts to support the Iraq sanctions, in 2005, OFAC fined Voices in the Wilderness $20,000 for giving medicines and other humanitarian supplies to Iraqis. In a similar case, OFAC imposed and attempted to collect a fine of $10,000, plus interest, against peace activist Bert Sacks for bringing medicines to Basra residents; [13] the charges against Sacks were dismissed by the court in December 2012.

In October 2007, a set of Spanish travel agency websites had their domain name access disabled by eNom: domain names had been blacklisted by OFAC. When asked, the U.S. Treasury referred to a 2004 press release stating that the company "had helped Americans evade travel restrictions to Cuba."

✓ Office of Intelligence and Analysis

The Office of Intelligence and Analysis is an agency of the U.S. Department of Homeland Security in charge of uniting and collating the information received from all relevant intelligence, counterintelligence, and field operations agencies in order to disseminate comprehensive reports to the Intelligence Community, state and local partners, and to the appropriate private sector. The agency is supervised by the Undersecretary of Security for Intelligence and Analysis. Its main objective is to identify the financial structures of terrorist groups and the vulnerabilities of the U.S. and world financial systems that can be exploited by terrorists.

IOW is also empowered to identify and attack the financial structures of networks engaged in the proliferation of weapons of mass destruction, organized crime groups and drug cartels.

This office is not restricted to FININT, but handles intelligence gathering, analysis and fusion throughout the Department. It disseminates intelligence information throughout the Department, to other members of the U.S. Intelligence Community, and to affected responders at state and local levels.

Depending on the specific federal violation, the police investigation may be under agencies including the Federal Bureau of Investigation, the U.S. Secret Service, or the Internal Revenue Service.

European Network of Financial Intelligence Units

The Financial Intelligence Unit Network (FIU.NET) is a decentralized computer network that provides an exchange of information between the financial intelligence units of the European Union. FIU.NET is a decentralized system without a central database where information is collected. All connected FIUs have their FIU.NET equipment within their own facilities and manage their own information. Through FIU.NET, connected FIUs create bilateral or multilateral cases. Match (autonomous, anonymous, analysis) is a matching tool within FIU.NET. The "match" makes it possible for FIUs to match names to find relevant data held by other connected FIUs. As the data is anonymized, the rules of privacy and data protection are not violated.

✓ Financial Intelligence Unit connected:

FIU.NET is funded by the European Commission and participating FIUs. Currently, the connected FIUs of the EU Member States are: Austria, Belgium, Bulgaria, Cyprus, Denmark, Estonia, Finland, France, Germany, Greece, Hungary, Ireland, Italy, Latvia, Lithuania, Luxembourg, Malta, Netherlands, Poland, Portugal, Romania, Sweden, Slovenia, Slovakia, Spain and the United Kingdom.

✓ Governing body

FIU.NET is governed by a Membership Board made up of connected FIUs, who have volunteered for a position. The Membership Board is chaired by an independent director.

✓ Project Management

The day-to-day operation of the system is managed by the FIU.NET Office, a project office of the Dutch Ministry of Security and Justice, which is located at Europol International Headquarters in The Hague.

Chapter II: Areas of understanding for financial intelligence

The four areas of understanding that make up financial intelligence are:

Understanding the foundation. Financial intelligence requires an understanding of the fundamentals of financial measurement, including the *income statement, balance sheet*, and *cash flow statement*. It also requires knowing the difference between cash and earnings and why a balance sheet is balanced.

- An income statement (also called a profit and loss statement, income statement, operating statement, or statement of operations) is one of a company's financial statements and shows the company's income and expenses for a given period.

  It indicates how revenues (also known as the "top line") are transformed into net profit (the result after all revenues and expenses have been posted). The purpose of the income statement is to show managers and investors whether the company made money (profits) or lost money (losses) during the reporting period.

The result statement can be prepared in one of two methods. The one-step income statement adds the income and subtracts the expenses to find the final result. The multi-step income statement takes several steps to get to the final result: starting with gross profit, then calculating operating expenses. Then, when it is deducted from the gross profit, the income from operations is obtained. The difference between other income and other expenses is added to the operating income. When combined with the operating income, the pre-tax income is obtained. The final step is to deduct the taxes, which ultimately produces the net income for the measured period.

- In financial accounting, a balance sheet or statement of financial situation is a summary of the financial statements of a person or organization, whether it is a sole proprietorship, a commercial partnership, a joint-stock company, a limited liability company, or another organization such as the government or a non-profit entity. Assets, liabilities and property are listed as of a specific date, such as the end of their financial year. A balance sheet is often described as a "snapshot of a company's financial situation." Of the four basic financial statements, the balance sheet is the only one that applies to a single point in time in a business calendar year.

A company's standard balance sheet has two sides: the asset side, on the left, and the financing side, which in turn has two parts, the liability side and the equity side, on the right. In general, the main categories of assets are listed first, and usually in order of liquidity. Assets are followed by liabilities. The difference between the asset and the liability is known as the equity or the net asset or the capital of the company and, according to the accounting equation, the equity must be equal to the asset minus the liability.

- In financial accounting, a cash flow statement is a financial statement that shows how changes in balance sheet accounts and income affect cash and cash equivalents, and breaks down the analysis into operating, investing and financing activities. Essentially, the cash flow statement refers to the cash flow in and out of the business. As an analytical tool, the cash flow statement is useful for determining the short-term viability of a company, in particular its ability to pay invoices. International Accounting Standard 7 (IAS 7) is the International Accounting Standard for cash flow statements.

Individuals and groups interested in cash flow statements include:

- o Accounting staff, who need to know if the organization will be able to cover payroll and other immediate expenses.

o   Lenders or potential creditors who want to have a clear idea of a company's ability to pay.

o   Potential investors, who need to judge whether the company is financially solid.

o   Potential employees or contractors who need to know if the company will be able to pay compensation.

o   Company directors, who are responsible for the governance of the company, and are responsible for ensuring that the company does not operate while it is insolvent.

o   Shareholders of the company.

Understanding art. Finance and accounting are an art and a science. The two disciplines should try to quantify what cannot always be quantified, and should therefore be based on rules, estimates and assumptions. Financial intelligence ensures that people are able to identify where the ingenious aspects of finance have been applied to numbers and knowing how to apply them differently can lead to different conclusions.

Understanding analysis. Financial intelligence includes the ability to analyze numbers in greater depth. This includes being able to calculate profitability, leverage, liquidity and the efficiency ratio, and understand the significance of results. Performing ROI analysis and interpreting the results is also part of financial intelligence.

Understanding the big picture. Financial intelligence also means being able to understand a company's financial results in context, that is, within the framework of the big picture. Factors such as the economy, the competitive environment, regulations and changing customer needs and expectations, as well as new technologies, influence the way figures are interpreted.

Financial intelligence is not just a theoretical learning. It also requires practice and application in the real world. In the corporate world, managers can show financial intelligence by speaking the language, i.e. asking questions about numbers when something doesn't make sense, reviewing financial reports and using information to understand the company's strengths and weaknesses, using return on investment (ROI) analysis, working capital management and ratio analysis to make decisions, and identifying where the art of finance has been applied.

Why is financial intelligence so important?

How did they raise you to think about money? For most people, much of what we learn about finances comes from our parents. For some, you had a good example to learn from. For others, you still have a lot to learn. Think about what you want to teach your kids about money. Sharon Lechter, an investor, business executive and mother, explains that today we face global and technological changes as big or even bigger than those that had been faced before. "No one can foresee the future, but one thing is certain: there are changes ahead that are beyond our reality. No matter what happens, we have two fundamental options: to go safe or to do it intelligently by preparing, educating and awakening your financial genius and that of your children."

One man who decided to play intelligently was Robert T. Kiyosaki, author of the book "Rich Father, Poor Father." At age 9, Robert became aware of financial inequality and decided to do something about it. He embarked on a journey that would forever change the course of his path. He took the one he least had transited, as his favorite poet, Robert Frost, wrote:

"Two roads diverged in a forest, and I, I took the least travelled. And that made all the difference."

Robert's father was very educated, had a considerable income, but had financial problems all his life and died leaving bills unpaid. Robert's best friend's father also had a substantial income, but he became one of Hawaii's richest men, and died leaving tens of millions of dollars to his family, charities and his church. The rich father of a friend of Robert taught him for a period of 30 years, starting at age 9. Choosing not to listen to the advice and attitude of his highly educated (poor) father about money was a painful decision, but it was one that shaped the rest of Robert's life. And that made all the difference.

Robert explains that one of the reasons the rich get richer, the poor get poorer, and the middle-class struggle over debt is because the subject of money is taught at home, not at school. Most of us learn about our parents' money. So, what can a poor father tell his son about money? They just say, "stay in school and study hard." The child can graduate with excellent grades, but with the mentality and financial programming of a poor person. In addition, schools focus on academic and professional skills, but not on financial skills. Robert explains that America's staggering national debt is largely due to highly educated politicians and government officials who make financial decisions with little or no training on the subject of money. How will a nation like the U.S. survive if teaching children about money is left in the hands of parents, most of whom will be or were already poor?

Robert learned this truth from his friend's rich father: if you learn the lessons of life, you'll do well. If not, life will continue to push you. People do two things. Some just let life push them. Others get angry and back off. But they reject their boss, or their job, or their spouse. They don't know its life that's pushing. Life pushes us. Some give up. Others fight. Some learn the lesson and move on. They welcome life by pushing them. For these few people, it means they need and want to learn something. They learn and move on. Most of them quit, and some of them fight. If you learn this lesson, you will become a wise, rich and happy person. If you don't, you will spend your life blaming your problems on a job, a low salary or your boss. Or if you're the kind of person who doesn't have the guts, you just give up every time life pushes you. You'll live your life playing it safe, doing the right thing, saving yourself for some event that will never happen. The truth is, you let life push you into submission. Deep down, you were terrified of taking risks. You really wanted to win, but the fear of losing was greater than the thrill of winning. This is the advice that Robert has taken with him when he embarked on his own path and became rich as a result.

THERE ARE 6 LESSONS ROBERT LEARNED FROM HIS FRIEND'S (RICH) DAD ABOUT MONEY:

LESSON #1: THE POOR AND MIDDLE-CLASS WORK FOR MONEY. THE RICH DON'T WORK FOR MONEY. THE RICH HAVE MONEY WORKING FOR THEM.

Just working for money jams people in the pattern of going to work to pay bills, and the more money they earn, the more they spend, so the cycle continues to work to pay bills. There are two emotions that drive them: desire and fear. To get out of the cycle, you must be honest, face the fear of not having money, use your mind and emotions to your advantage, delay your reactions and think on your own. Being rich doesn't solve the problem. There are rich people who are still bound by fear, afraid of losing their wealth. The joy that money brings is of short duration. You must master the power of money, not be afraid of it or be a slave to it. The way to do this is to choose what you think instead of reacting to emotions.

The main cause of poverty or financial struggle is fear and ignorance, not the economy, the government or the rich. The life of a human is a struggle between ignorance and enlightenment. Once a person stops looking for information and self-knowledge, ignorance arises. That struggle is a decision from moment to moment: to learn to open or close the mind.

That's how you let the money work for you:

- o Don't spend your life living in fear.

- o Never stop exploring your dreams.

- o Avoid working hard for money.

- o Avoid thinking that money will buy you things that will make you happy.

- o Don't let money run your life.

- o See the opportunities that others miss.

- o Start a business that makes money, even when you're not there.

Never stop using your mind and imagination to identify an opportunity to earn money. You will see opportunities that others will miss because they are looking for money and security.

LESSON #2: IF YOU WANT TO BE RICH AND MAINTAIN YOUR WEALTH, IT IS IMPORTANT TO BE TRAINED IN FINANCE, IN BOTH WORDS, AS WELL AS IN NUMBERS.

In life, it's not about how much money you make, it's about how much money you keep. Money without financial intelligence is money that leaves soon. It is more important to work to educate yourself financially than to worry about money. The greatest wealth is financial education.

Rule: you must know the difference between an asset and a liability. An asset is something that puts money in my pocket. A liability is something that takes money out of my pocket. If you want to be rich, just spend your life buying assets. If you want to be poor or middle class, spend your life buying liabilities. It's not knowing the difference that makes most of the financial struggle in the real world.

Robert admits that he is still challenged by the idea that a house is not an asset. Why is a house not an asset?

1. Most people work their whole lives paying for a house they never own.

2. Although people receive a tax deduction for interest on mortgage payments, they pay all their other expenses with after-tax dollars.

3. Property taxes.

4. Houses don't always rise in value.

5. The greatest losses of all are those of missed opportunities. If all your money is tied up in your home, you may be forced to work harder because your money continues to go to expenses, rather than potential assets.

This doesn't mean I don't buy a house. It is important to understand the difference between an asset and a liability. If you want to buy a larger home, you must first purchase assets that will generate the cash flow to pay for the home. The rich get richer because of their assets.

LESSON #3: TO BE FINANCIALLY SECURE, A PERSON NEEDS TO MAINTAIN HIS/HER OWN BUSINESS.

There's a big difference between your profession and your business. One problem with school is that you often become what you study. The mistake of becoming what you study is that many people forget to mind their own business. They spend their lives taking care of someone else's business and enriching it. To be financially secure, a person needs to mind their own business. Your business revolves around your assets, rather than your income. The rich focus on their assets, while everyone else focuses on their income statements. The main reason most poor and middle-class people are financially conservative and don't take risks is because they don't have a financial base. How do you start running your own business?

- Keep up your daily work but start buying real assets.

- Keep your expenses low, reduce liabilities.

- What are assets? The following include several categories:

- Businesses that don't require my presence.

- Actions

- Bonds.

- Investment funds.

- Revenue-generating real estate.

- Notes (promissory notes).

- Intellectual property royalties such as music, scripts, patents.

- Anything else that has value, produces income or is appreciated and has a market ready.

LESSON #4: UNDERSTAND THE HISTORY OF TAXES AND CORPORATIONS.

The real reality is that the rich don't pay taxes. It is the middle class that pays for the poor, especially the high-income educated middle class. The rich don't deliver, they react. They have money, power and intention of changing things. Not only do they voluntarily pay more taxes. They're looking for ways to minimize their tax burden. They hire smart lawyers and accountants and persuade politicians to change laws or create loopholes. They have the resources to effect change. The poor and the middle class do not have the same resources.

Financial intelligence is the synergy of many skills and talents. But it's the combination of 4 technical skills that are the basis of financial intelligence. Financial intelligence includes these areas of expertise:

o   Financial education. Accounting. The ability to read numbers.

o   Investing. The science of money by making money.

o   Understand markets. Supply and demand.

o   The Law. Awareness of corporate, state and national accounting rules and regulations.

If you aspire to a great wealth, it is the combination of these skills that will greatly amplify your financial intelligence.

In a nutshell - The rich who own corporations:

1. They win.

2. They spend.

3. They pay taxes.

People who work for corporations:

1. They win.

2. They pay taxes.

3. They spend.

LESSON #5: THE RICH INVENT MONEY. THEY SEE OPPORTUNITY WHERE OTHERS DON'T.

One thing in common in all of us: we all have a tremendous potential, and we are all blessed with gifts. However, what holds us all back is a certain degree of self-doubt. Some are more affected than others.

Financial intelligence is simply having more options. It's not so much what happens, but how many different financial solutions you can come up with to turn one lemon into millions. It's how creative you are at solving financial problems. Most people only know one solution: work hard, save and borrow. Then why increase their financial intelligence? However, others want to take what happens and make it better. They create luck. That's how money is. If you want to be luckier and make money instead of working hard, then your financial intelligence is important. If you're waiting for the right thing to happen, you can wait for a long time. What is money, after all? It's what we agreed it is. If you can understand the idea that money isn't real, you'll get rich faster. The most powerful asset we all have is our mind. If you train well, you can create enormous seemingly instant wealth.

Money is invented, created and protected using financial intelligence.

Great opportunities are not seen with your eyes. You see them with your mind. You need to be financially trained to recognize the opportunities in front of you.

How to invest wisely?

1. Find opportunities that others lose. Look with your mind at what others miss with their eyes.

2. Learn how to raise money. It's what you know more than what you buy. Investing is not buying, it's a matter of knowing.

3. Learn how to organize smart people. Intelligent people work or hire a person who is smarter than he is. When you need advice, choose wisely.

LESSON #6: WORK TO LEARN - NOT WORK FOR MONEY.

Unfortunately, today, the sad truth is that great talent is not enough. When it comes to money, the only skill most people know is to work hard. Robert's friend's rich father said: "You want to know a little about a lot of things." Safety at work meant everything to Robert's educated father, learning meant everything to his friend's rich father. Robert recommends that young people look for work because of what they are going to learn, more than they are going to earn. See along the way what skills you want to acquire before choosing a specific profession and before getting caught up in the "Rat Race". The "Rat Race" is the pattern of getting up, going to work, paying bills, getting up, going to work, paying bills. Being trapped in the trap of paying bills for life is like the little hamsters that run on metal wheels. Robert invented a game called Cashflow, which is a fun but educational board game that teaches you how to get out of the rat race and into the fast lane of life, where your assets exceed your obligations.

It's important that you prepare for success. This means learning all aspects of business systems. This means working as several companies, to gain a wide variety of experience, learning and skills. The management skills necessary for success are:

1. Cash flow management.

2. Systems management (including you and time with your family).

3. People management.

The most important specialized skills are sales and marketing understanding. The ability to sell (communicate with another person) is the basic skill of personal success. It is communication skills such as writing, speaking and negotiating that are crucial to a successful life. The better you communicate, negotiate and manage your fear of rejection, the easier your life will be. We also need to be good teachers and good students. To be truly rich, we need to be able to give and receive. Giving money is the secret for most big rich families. The most important law of money: "Give and you shall receive."

10 reasons why financial intelligence is the key to success

Financial intelligence sounds like something only a few chosen people own, but in reality, there is a little of it in all of us. The difference is that we are not all aware of it, and there are even those who do not know how to use it for their maximum benefit. Some people have it more than others and have a sharper view of how to use their money to make more money. Experts in the field will tell you that there are no top secrets or quick fixes to getting rich. That doesn't mean you have to try too hard either.

You just need to understand it better and start making changes in the way you handle money.

You probably won't find someone successful who isn't aware of financial intelligence either. This is regardless of how you want to define success. You may not have a lot of cash, but you're happy with what you work with and what comes out of it. This can be considered a success. In the same way, you can have a lot of money, but be wasteful and waste it on anything until it runs out, and that could be classified as unsuccessful.

So, let's analyze so as you know exactly what financial intelligence is and why it's so important to have it, and how it can change your life.

The good news is that this kind of intelligence is an ability to learn. Basically, it's about knowing the ins and outs of a financial situation, whether it's your personal finances, the finances of your company or a company you work for. Basically it means to understand and acquire knowledge and skills in finance in the business world. It is relatively a new term that has gained increasing popularity to help people to increase financial results, decrease employee turnover by including employees in financial decisions within companies.

1. Increase your wealth

Is there anyone who doesn't want to increase their wealth? For business-minded people, the most important thing to know is the cash flow. Whether you own a business or not, you need to know where your money is going. One of the reasons rich people get rich and rich is because they have their eyes on the cash flow and control it all the time. You don't have to own a business to keep track of where your money is going, nor do you have to be making a lot of money to keep an eye on it. Once you know your cash flow, you'll find out where the money is going that can be modified, diminished or cut back completely. This will automatically increase your money.

2. How it relates to money

You may not believe it, but the way you think about money has a lot to do with financial intelligence and the success you can have. We all know the old saying, "money is the root of all evil." Some of us were educated to believe that, while others were educated with an "easy come, easy go" attitude. While others were educated to believe that they have to work hard for their money and that "money does not grow on trees". Whatever your belief, the only thing we should all believe and be convinced of is that money can be controlled.

Successful people control money, not the other way around. They decide where he's going or who he's going to go to. Your relationship with money should expand and not be limited to what you learned when you were young. Formal education doesn't really address the issue of money this way, and unless you've specialized in finance, neither does college. So, don't take anything you've learned about money to the letter.

3. What do you know about money?

There's a difference between your belief in money and what you know about money. Now, for many of us, we only know the purchasing power of money, and that's where our knowledge ends. To make use of financial intelligence, we need to know more. We need to understand how money works or what the assets are versus our liabilities. Many of us don't know the difference between a credit card and a debit card. Lack of knowledge is what often forces us to make financial mistakes that lead to indebtedness or a bad financial investment, which can also lead to indebtedness.

There are many tools that help us increase our knowledge of finance, and it's just a matter of using them. If you're a library mouse, read more about finance. There are more than a pile of books, articles and blogs on how to increase your financial intelligence. If you're more of an audiovisual student, watch programs and interviews with experts who explain the corners and cracks you don't know. There are even applications that will make it easier for you to learn financially by tracking your spending habits.

4. What you do with money

Raise your hand if you think you're doing too little. Most of us think we make very little money and that's why we're always in financial trouble. However, it is true that no matter how much we earn, we never think it is enough. This is because the more you earn, the more you start spending. Then it becomes a race between what is earned and what is spent, and we know that what is spent always brings out the best in us and wins. But what you're spending on is that question you definitely need to ask yourself.

At least we've heard of the "From Poverty to Wealth" story. We've read real stories about people who came from nowhere to something big. And we've read about the opposite, of the people who spent all their money and ended up as a poor homeless. These stories are not just for entertainment; they are lessons to learn from. They intend to show you that success does not depend on how much you earn, but rather on what you do with those earnings. A simple example of what many financially savvy people do is save at least 10% of their income automatically. They never see that 10%. They use that percentage for future investment purposes or keep it for long-term gain.

5. What is the best investment option?

That's a popular question for people. Should I invest in real estate? Stocks? Bonds? These and more can be good investments, but not before you invest in yourself. This is the best investment you can make at any time in your life. When you do that, you're much more likely to get the success you want. That's why people take courses in a multitude of subjects, for example. The person who is going to make your wealth grow is you, so developing yourself is something worth the time and effort.

When you focus on self-development, you'll know what you're good at and what you can succeed at. For many people, personal development changed their entire life and lifestyle. People have given up their careers to other types of work or investments and have had total success in areas they had never thought they would be in. This can happen because the mentality has changed, making people more enlightened.

6. Control what you can

There are many things that are not in our hands. It's not in our hands how the stock market is acting. It's not in our hands whether real estate goes down or up. Your salary, even if it comes into your hands, is not in your hands. With so many things not under our control, it's easy to despair. But you need to focus on what you can control. What you want to invest in, it's under your control. The way you spend your salary is also under your control.

Today, we live in a world of very rapid change and the future will always be full of uncertainties. But financially savvy people know that what they do today, will affect their tomorrow. Try to fine-tune your outlook and realize that every financial step you take today will have a positive or negative impact on the future.

7. Hire financially savvy people

Without intelligence, not only will your money not last, but you won't even be able to do it in the first place. It's easy to believe you don't have the ability to be financially smart. You're not alone in this. Actually, it's part of intelligence to know that you don't know everything. And although most of us have it within us, we still don't know how to use that intelligence to make it work for us.

If you're really lost, there's nothing wrong with paying someone to help you understand and shed some light on the subject. Yes, you'd rather have free advice, but that free advice from someone you know could lead you to pay a high price later if that advice is incorrect.

8.   Short- and long-term goals

You probably have short-term goals you want to achieve; we all do. You need to differentiate them from your short-term goals, as that will keep you focused and balanced. Both are money goals. However, we usually get caught up in the short term and forget the long term for a long time. It is not possible to say enough that so many people are better off spending money than doing it right. And this is because we don't have an action plan in place. You need to protect your future and your wealth and use or invest your money in things that will also serve to your long-term goals.

There are insurance blogs available, reviewing the pros and cons of Guaranteed Universal Life Insurance. This could be an investment you could consider helping you reach your long-term goal. At any given time, after a lifetime of work, you will want to rest or retire and enjoy your time and live well and make sure everything is being cared for by professionals in the life insurance business.

9. Learn more

When you expand your network of people to include people who are financially intelligent, it will help you even more. When people want advice on financial matters, they tend to talk to someone they trust, but they may not know much more than you, or they may even know less than you do about money matters. He's a kind of blind man leading a blind man who definitely won't help you achieve future success. You need people who are in the field, who manage and understand money well. The wider your network, the greater the advantage you gain by learning new things and acquiring good money habits.

10. The guilt game

The last point to mention is our love for the guilt game. We blame our work, our boss, our family, our circumstances, the weather and our dogs and cats for why our money seems to disappear. A big part of financial intelligence is making us men and women and being responsible for our own mistakes with money. We cannot succeed if we do not admit our faults and limitations and do something about them.

Intelligence solves problems, not money

This is good, because it's in your hands to boost your financial intelligence. When you push it through what we've been talking about, the money will go up too. This is the time to think like a businessman, even if you're not. Track yourself, your expenses and change your way of thinking or at least expand it, understand more about money and ask people, the right questions to put you on the right path to success.

Chapter III: What is financial intelligence analysis? From a defensive to a proactive approach

Risk management is not just about financial transactions, but about abstract relationships connected through commerce and carried out by those who do their best to appear to be completely legitimate. What is financial intelligence analysis? It is a valuable intelligence and risk management tool that can be used for both a defensive and a proactive approach.

The defensive approach

What is financial intelligence analysis? One of the main objectives of financial intelligence is "to identify financial transactions that may involve tax evasion, money laundering or any other criminal activity." Defensive financial intelligence analysis activities protect the organization by identifying risky behaviors (the customer making large investments without the funds to back them up) and suspicious transactions (such as those with blacklisted countries or organizations) before they have a chance to harm the business. A defensive approach is important, but it is only part of a sound financial intelligence strategy.

The proactive approach

A strategic and proactive approach to financial intelligence analysis gives users greater decision-making power to protect their assets from risk and fraud. A proactive approach involves a unified view of information at the speed of real-time events. Allows intercepting weak signals and trends before they become reality.

Monitoring activities, for competitors and market trends, are able to exploit all kinds of financial data and news flows for their intelligence value. By automatically extracting and correlating this information that would otherwise be impossible to analyze manually, analysts can choose whether to modify their investment decisions or to choose with whom to do business early or how to do it.

Cognitive technology for financial analysis

In short, we can say that financial intelligence analysis provides the financial knowledge you need to protect or add value to your business. The problem is, how can we collect, understand and analyze the mass of information needed (structured or unstructured, qualitative or quantitative, traditional or less common, hidden or easy to detect, inside or outside the organization) for our analysis?

This is where Cogito's cognitive technology can help. Cogito enables financial organizations to take full advantage of information to make quick, informed decisions about portfolio and investment strategies. With cognitive capabilities based on artificial intelligence algorithms that mimic the human ability to read and understand, Cogito makes large amounts of content easily and immediately accessible, enriches quantitative analysis methods, and develops customized sensors that constantly monitor information flows.

In this way, Cogito can reduce the risk of illegal financial activities and, at the same time, help extract strategic value from the information for decision making.

What is the Financial Intelligence Analysis Unit?

The Financial Intelligence Analysis Unit (FIAU) is a government agency that has been created in accordance with Malta's obligation to combat money laundering and terrorist financing. A job in this Unit is a specialized job that requires specific technical and analytical knowledge. These apply in relation to the basic functions of the Unit, which include the detailed analysis of suspicious transaction reports submitted to it from time to time. When circumstances warrant it, the results of the analytical exercise are sent to the Police for investigation of the parties listed in the Suspicious Transaction Reports.

- **Roles and responsibilities**

The Financial Intelligence Analysis Unit acts as Malta's FIU and is the designated entity to fulfil the responsibilities of an FIU as set out in the Third European Union Directive on Money Laundering (Directive 2005/60/EC) and in the 40 FATF Recommendations.

The specific responsibilities of the Unit are detailed in Article 16 of the Money Laundering Prevention Act. These include the following:

- **Financial Analysis**

The Financial Analysis Section is tasked with receiving and analyzing Suspicious Transaction Reports (SARs) and collecting information in response to international requests for information received from foreign FIUs. When an STR is received, the Section conducts a thorough case analysis and prepares an analytical report. This is then presented to the Financial Analysis Committee to determine whether dissemination of information to the Police should be made on the basis of a reasonable suspicion of money laundering or terrorist financing. For purposes of analysis, the Unit is empowered to require information from any natural or legal person, including those subjects to the Money Laundering and Terrorist Financing Regulations.

Financial analysts are also responsible for gathering information on financial and commercial activities in

Malta in order to detect areas that could be vulnerable to money laundering or terrorist financing. The Section's ongoing compilation and maintenance of comprehensive statistics and records also helps FIAU to identify threats and assess risks at the national level.

- **Compliance Monitoring**

The primary function of the Compliance Section is the supervision and monitoring of compliance by the persons subject (including Financial Institutions and Designated Non-Financial Businesses and Professions), based on the evolution of internal procedures for on-site examinations and off-site monitoring. Onsite assessments are conducted by the compliance officers or supervisory authorities involved, who act on behalf of the FIAU. In both cases, the Unit is responsible for preparing the relevant compliance reports, which include a list of corrective actions deemed necessary.

Compliance Officers are also actively involved in providing training to officers of subject persons and assisting subject persons to develop effective AML/CFT measures and programs. They also monitor developments in the methods, typologies and trends of money laundering and terrorist financing in order to provide guidance and feedback by transmitting up-to-date information to the persons concerned.

- **Legal and International Relations**

The Legal and International Relations Section is responsible for overseeing the international aspects of FIAU's functions and providing legal advice to the various Sections of the Unit. In addition to the drafting of legal instruments and implementing procedures, the staff of this section is also tasked with responding to legal queries from affected persons. This section also oversees the exchange of information with foreign FIUs and both domestic and foreign supervisory authorities, including the conclusion of Memoranda of Understanding.

- **Distribution of the organization**

The Board of Governors is responsible for the policy to be adopted by the Unit, which is to be executed and implemented by the Director, and for ensuring that the Director implements it accordingly. The Board is also responsible for advising the Minister on all matters and issues pertaining to the prevention, detection, analysis, investigation, prosecution and conviction of money laundering and terrorist financing ("ML/FT") offences.

The Director is responsible for carrying out the operations and functions of FIAU and for executing the policies established by the Board of Directors. The director is assisted by permanent staff organized into various sections/departments, which are:

1. The **Financial Analysis** section which is composed of financial analysts who are

responsible for the receipt and analysis of suspicious transaction reports ("STRs") and the dissemination of analytical and other financial reports.

2. The **Compliance** Section which is responsible for monitoring compliance by persons with the relevant anti-money laundering and anti-money laundering legislation and terrorist financing ("AML/CFT") provisions under the MLPA, the PMLFTR and the FIAU Implementation Procedures.

3. The **Legal and International Relations** Section, which advises the Unit, assists in subjecting persons through the provision of training and guidance on legal matters and manages the Unit's international affairs.

4. **The Corporate Services** section, whose staff members are responsible for the unit's administrative and accounting matters.

5. **The Information Technology and Information Security** Section, whose staff manages the information technology configuration of the Unit.

6. **The Quality Assurance and Policy** Section, which is responsible for conducting reviews and audits of the operations of the various sections of the Unit, as well as ensuring compliance with work methodologies, policies and procedures.

Conclusion

We hope that this guide can turn you into an entrepreneur and that you will learn and develop financial intelligence, which is a compilation of information about the financial affairs of entities of interest, to understand their nature and capabilities, and to predict their intentions. Read, don't be alone with this information, get trained, invest in knowledge that is an investment that pays off in the short, medium and long term, and the most important thing is that it is for life. Become a master of the money game to build true financial freedom in business.

Strive and dedicate yourself to create and persistently carry a budget and stick to it, which is one of the most important decisions in financial planning in a personal, family or any business. Make an estimate of income, a prediction of expenses and an allocation of resources. It is a tool that is considered indispensable to know in which direction you are going, or how your family is doing when it comes to the economic and financial field, or how the monetary life of your business is going and what you will do or must do to achieve your goals and objectives. It's like plotting the route on a map, detailing the cost of each leg to the final destination and how to finance the trip.

Invest in assets, not just in liabilities. Investing in real assets should be the number one rule for you and your family when you are thinking about where to put your savings or those of the company. Don't let fear and poor financial education make you think that the safest and most ideal place for your savings is a checking account or a deposit that won't generate any extra income. Throughout history it has been shown that having money in an account, in a deposit or under a slab or bed, in the long term deteriorates our purchasing power, precisely because you do not add more than you save and as we know, over time money is devalued.

Remember, if you don't know how to educate yourself, how to organize yourself or your company economically, use an expert. Don't go to your friend, who tastes the same or less than you. When you don't know what knowledge, you should acquire or what new skills to learn, research and/or hire a specialist. We all continue to need help from others to meet our needs and problems.

Bibliographic References

Editorial Nóstica (2018. Financial Intelligence for All: A
Practical Guide to Managing Your Money.
Retrieved from
https://books.google.com.pe/books?id=3HCiv
QEACAAJq=libros+from+intelligence+financi
al&hl=en&sa=X&ved=0ahUKEwjMwcTg_5vl
AhVNnKwKHetYDGgQ6AEIKDAA

Kiyosaki, R. (2012). Increase your financial IQ.
Retrieved from
https://books.google.com.pe/books?id=ZHsM
CLtRSZ8Crintsec=frontcoverq=libros+from+i
ntelligence+financial&hl=en&sa=X&ved=0ah
UKEwjMwcTg_5vlAhVNnKwKHetYDGgQ6
AEINjAC#v=onepage&q=books%20of%20int
elligence%20financial&f=false

Kiyosaki, R. (2018). Rich Dad, Poor Dad: What The
Rich Teach Their Kids About Money.
Recuperado de
https://books.google.com.pe/books?id=Cx6a
DwAAQBAJ&printsec=frontcover&dq=libros
+de+inteligencia+financiera&hl=en&sa=X&ve
d=0ahUKEwjMwcTg_5vlAhVNnKwKHetYD
GgQ6AEILzAB#v=onepage&q&f=false

Borghino, M. (2012). The art of making money (The art of). Retrieved from https://books.google.com.pe/books?id=DzrSl XvBGKYCrintsec=frontcoverq=libros+de+int eligencia+financiera&hl=en&sa=X&ved=0ahU KEwjMwcTg_5vlAhVNnKwKHetYDGgQ6A EIWzAH#v=onepage&q=libros%20de%20int eligencia%20financiera&f=false

Karen Berman. (2007). Finance for managers: Fundamental concepts of finance for non-financials. Retrieved from https://books.google.com.pe/books?id=HJDk GY8eKdICg=PA31q=libros+de+inteligencia+ financiera&hl=en&sa=X&ved=0ahUKEwi6pZ CqgZzlAhUQS60KHelSD3E4ChDoAQg3MAI #v=onepage&q=libros%20de%20inteligencia% 20financiera&f=false

Lightning Source UK Ltd.
Milton Keynes UK
UKHW022159160622
404555UK00009B/88

9 781647 772666